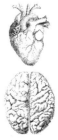

Trying to Be a Person
Wesley Scott McMasters

WORDS DANCE PUBLISHING
WordsDance.com

1st Edition
ISBN-13: 978-0-9979404-0-4
ISBN-10: 0-9979404-0-9

Coffee Art by Isaac Samay
Cover photo, design & interior layout by Amanda Oaks

Type set in Bergamo & Albertsthal Typewriter

Words Dance Publishing
WordsDance.com

In memory of Scott McMasters Jr.

Trying to Be a Person
Wesley Scott McMasters

Trying to Be a Person

20-Somethings Who Say "Namaste" at Whole Foods; or, Trying to Be a Person

I won't say that I'm a prototypical hipster
but I drink PBR because I like it

oh

okay

     I don't look for the divine
          next to bulk granola

     but if I ever decide to

maybe I'll learn something

     because
     the places I've looked
     just make me miss
     sunshine on skin
     and my grandfather

and sometimes the divine is only visible
after midnight

when the needle is still spinning
but no music is playing
and you don't have the energy
to turn it off

New Orleans Architecture

vines crawl up the side of
the old brick building
where I read poems about
           sex
           and a novel about the letter V

and I realized
on a 10 hour drive
that Maine interstates don't have billboards

there's something beautiful about that
        but I don't like pine trees

and your phone call
about visiting me in Tampa
        made me smile
        and you kissed me in an airport
before you went back to the city
and found a boyfriend

who will wear a J.Crew scarf to match yours

I'm sorry darling but that's not me

I'll still love you in a way that will make you always wonder
        whether I really do or not

because that's the appeal to you
isn't it

and here's my secret

I'll never know myself if I loved you or not
        and I never kissed you in New Orleans
        under one of those gaslight lampposts

and my fingers will never crawl up your side
        or learn the curve of your neck

instead
I'll become some artifact
     a pressed flower in a book

that you forgot was there
until you opened it up
     to your favorite passage

Margot and the Nuclear So-Sos Sometimes Plays When I'm in the Local Coffee Shop, but this Poem Is Not about One of Their Songs

for Nadia

a song by someone
I can't pronounce the name of

reminds me of a red dress

and the first time I danced
when I was 16
somewhere
in Vienna

and now
how a red sweater
falls on your hips

DAILY AFFIRMATION

this is my daily affirmation
today I am beautiful
I feel better
today I embrace my differences
today I embrace my spirituality

today I remember promises you made
I remember promises you broke
I remember things you didn't do

I remember what I didn't do
I remember thinking that being in love was a thing

today I remember
whether I want to forget or not

I remember in a rainstorm
standing under an eave
trying to understand

what you said to me

how you explained what you had done
and how you explained what I should do
and how we should be
while you still looked beautiful

more beautiful than ever
in that terrible moment
only a minimal feeling at first, but then

today I remember family dinners
I remember feeling fucked up
I remember feeling that I was wrong

I remember feeling that I was a weird kid
unable to fit in
unable to match
unable to be liked

and somehow I made it
somehow I forgot all of that

forgot might be a strong word

today I am no longer sitting at a lunch table
wondering what I did wrong
or what was wrong with me

today I no longer feel bad for
not being what I was expected to be
for not having the qualities that might have been preferred
for having the interests that would have made life easier

today I remember that I'm scared to death

and today I remember that Icarus also flew
and that you told me about that poem
when it was tattooed around a pomegranate
on your ribcage
years after you left me for Italy

and I just read the poem again the other day
and I understood it this time

and I'm scared half to death

and here I am

today I am here
today I have forgotten that kind of pain
today you can stand behind me

because today I am powerful
today I do what you think I cannot

today I do what I think I cannot

today I disturb the Universe

today I hold planets in my back pocket
and your hand in mine

whom do I talk to?
is it you whom I ask for forgiveness?

don't flatter yourself

I need forgiveness from myself and my God
and I'll be lucky to get one of those

[Untitled]

I felt a crash
and I saw the other car upside down
someone's life
exiting
the body

steam flowing from a hot pot of tea
screaming
screeching
echoing
yelling
in pain
in exultation
in something that I do not understand

I walked away from a crumpled mass of metal
twisted and jarred
glass shattered on the ground
like when I was a teenager
trying to make art
by reassembling broken pieces of glass

now with no shoes
and asking the questions
that I didn't want to know the answers to

I didn't sleep that night
discharged from the hospital with a bottle
of ibuprofen
that I couldn't take
because my stomach was empty

I thought I waited to see the news
in the morning

which read like the event replayed in my mind

a car speeding out of nowhere

hitting another from behind
one flying into a guardrail
the other into a tree

one dead
three taken to the hospital

but I wasn't waiting to see the news

I watched the sun come up that morning
with a cup of coffee
in a hand that wasn't broken
standing with legs that were intact

in a body that was somehow whole

but the inside of my body
felt like those pieces of glass
shattered all over the place

maybe they had been broken all along and
I just noticed for the first time

and I found myself trying to reassemble the pieces

For AJ; Or Why I Still Rock My Khakis with a Cuff and a Crease

once you said
I am home- we live here

and you were right
because I see you and me and everyone

with arms spread out
fingers apart
like the roots of an oak tree

yeah a lot like the oak tree I used to climb in my
grandmother's back yard when I was a kid

and these roots that spread out into the air around us
hanging on desperately

like the roots of that oak tree
before it got pulled out violently to make room for a garage

and I see our fingers extending and reaching out and rooting into
these spaces
because they pull you in and latch on
and when I go to visit my grandparents
my roots fit neatly into the grooves in the dirt-air

that the roots of my grandparents made

which are the same paths
that the roots from my father made
when he came back from Alaska
with the exact opposite of a tan

and I reach out and my finger-roots breathe in the dirt-air
and I know that I am home
and easily so

but when I am here
I reach out

and as long as there is something for me to hold on to
then I am also home

and when I stand and I look at the trees change leaves
in the spot where my mother took me to watch them

for the first time

my finger-roots fit in the easiest

and you don't have finger-roots
you are the tree
and you hold those around you
with Christmas lights

and an airplane bottle of Canadian Club just in case it's a long night

and you will not be violently ripped away
because I know you
and I know what you said that one time

we are home

and you were right

and so when I reach my finger-roots out
they pass by yours

when the finger-roots reach in to fill those familiarly worn places
I breathe in deep and remember
and also breathe in deep to forget

3 Haiku for Late October

Water boils for tea;
my mother watches a bird
rest, weary from flight

I shiver from air
felt around the window pane;
frost in the corner

A fire is built
with wood stacked since September
neatly under eaves

The Four Blood Moons

Moon 1

Joel said the moon
would turn red
and the Lord would return

would I remain
to inherit a world that I
understood

would be left for the meek

Moon 2

perhaps the prophecy promises
a new age

maybe the moon
signals a rebirth

and maybe in this world
our wrongs will be made right

maybe Johnny Depp will stop making Pirates of the Caribbean movies

maybe Donald Trump will end his campaign

maybe my students will want to learn about poetry

maybe an atom bomb will not exist

and maybe the Gaza Strip will become like Siberia
        cold and a little unwanted

maybe there would not have been a Boondock Saints sequel

maybe I can walk into the supermarket and buy what I want
        with my good looks

maybe people will realize that blaring the music in your headphones
doesn't actually make you look as cool as you think it does

I could drink all the beer and eat all the pizza I wanted
I would have gotten into the cab when she asked me to

I would have lived in Philadelphia

maybe disease wouldn't exist

and age wouldn't cripple

and maybe you could buy Bulleit bourbon for the price of Old Crow

or you wouldn't have to change your email password every 180 days

but I am no prophet
and here is no great matter

Moon 3

if a cool night
          on a parkbench
elevated
in Greenwich Village

was paradise
          then I think

I would be okay with that

Moon 4

Joel said the moon
would turn red
and the Lord would return

and would I remain
and inherit a world I
understood

would be left for the meek

and if this signals the end of times
as I begin to feel the air of Autumn
on my face and I smell the leaves
that remind me of riding in my grandfather's truck
on the way to the movies
windows down
a pack of cigarettes which will eventually kill him
on the seat in between us

I don't want to be remembered as meek anymore

[Untitled]

I see your shadow
    it lingers somewhere in the corner

under a pile of clothes
    a pair of worn jeans that are tight on the thighs
and a black t-shirt with a band on it that I haven't
    listened to in at least three years

I breathe your shadow in
    and when it comes out
as a cloud of vapor

I know that I've used my lungs
    for every purpose
but breathing

and if the din of a crowd
    and the slowed rhythm of a song
is anything like dying
I would be quite surprised

when a bird drifts slowly and alone
    I remember silence
and a tea kettle

I remember a dream of God and the Devil

and I wonder when we will run out of room for the dead

and where we will go
    because I'm not sure Stanley Kubrick's 2001: A Space Odyssey
    answers all of my questions

because being storm-tossed off the coast of Montauk Point
    must feel the same
    as standing alone for the first time
with a Greyhound driving away in the distance
taking somebody with it
    and it's probably raining

and there's a lamppost standing behind me
casting just enough light
    for my shadow to stretch sideways
    halfway to you

Girls with Coins — open mic

some girls drink whiskey
for the taste

or to say "Manhattan"

but you drink it to get fucked up

like it was meant to be drunk

and you listen to songs
furiously
like a fire
under your undancing feet

and sometimes I recall a painting
in a corner
of a museum in a city I loved
standing with a girl I loved more
and I never understood

she was a red chaos
like a child's furious wall scribble
passed off
as modern art

but what I see now

is a heel waiting to be cut
a painting misunderstood
and something
lost

Upon Listening to Tool's "Hooker with a Penis"

I've stood at the edge of the porch at my family home

the home I grew up in
filled with memories of variable sorts

and I have nothing to hide behind
in front of the same sky I stood in front of as a four year old child
for the first time
birds crying in historical echo
my parents smiling behind me
proud of building something

(but let me foreshadow: time can heal as well as destroy)

the same birds now calling to me to remember something

and I've heard that remembrance of things past is desirable

but I've never read Proust and I don't plan to

I can say this

each bird's song in the early morning during the first warm days of
spring is a memory that refuses to be forgotten

I have fought to forget

I've fought to be washed clean of these mistakes
and feel a wind in my hair from the only time
I enjoyed being on the beach
early in the morning
a Hemingway novel under my thirteen year old arm
that was just beginning to do push ups
and my grandfather

healthy
fishing in the roaring surf
and a gray sky as a backdrop

not as I see him now
with an oxygen tank holding him down
3 X 3 pills 3 times a day

quick to anger
quick to sadness
always forgetting

and someone that I'm terrified to say goodbye to

when I say that I'm terrified to lose him
I'll have you understand
that it won't be a month to be near me

sometimes I'll hear a seagull
because
each bird's song in the early morning during the first warm days of
spring is a memory that refuses to be forgotten

and if I reach out my hand to you
will you remember
what my favorite dessert is?

because if love works the way that it does in my family
I'm not sure I know what it is

but I know it can be hard

and I crossed the Mississippi for the first time regretfully
because life changes when you wake up in someone else's bed

and I spent most of college sleeping on couches
waking up on the floor in the corner
or next to someone who would learn to despise me

because I'm insecure
and need to feel wanted
in ways that my father would assure me
are for people with less resolve

and in California the seagulls sound different
and the tacos are okay

I much prefer the southern part of the Mississippi
and I wish this was in iambic pentameter
so you could hear my rhythm
and understand that everything that I do
is somehow an echo of you
and an echo of everything I want to remember
and do you hear the cadence in my voice
when I tell you what you mean to me?

like the time I walked around Walden pond with my mother

and the time my father took me into the woods and explained
that I needed to drag my feet
and listen for the rattle of a snake

and like the time that
early in the morning
a Hemingway novel under my thirteen year old arm
that was just beginning to do push ups
and my grandfather

healthy
fishing in the roaring surf
and a gray sky as a backdrop

and here I am
waiting for these birds

my God is a ghost that lingers like a fog settled
over everything at first light
but dissipates with time
as brightness distracts

every moment when the air has a chill
and a woman brushes close by me

with the smell of a cigarette
mixed with cheap perfume

I fall for a girl from college again
who had a side tattoo and a tongue ring

a bad sense of humor and a taste for horror movies

but I'd rather smell coffee in the morning
as the birds begin to call out

like when a fever breaks
but then I have to consider that

each bird's song in the early morning during the first warm days of
spring is a memory that refuses to be forgotten

A Romance in Three Parts

Part I:

we used to get together
on Friday nights
after the football games

and smoke cigarettes
under the bleachers

shivering
and staring
at the moon

Part II:

three years later
I drove by
her house on
Tuesday nights
after work and
Friday nights
with whiskey warming me
and Saturday mornings
just for fun

and I threw
my empty Marlboro boxes
out of the
hand cranked window
of my '95 Chevy

just so that bitch knew
how I felt

Part III:

I'm shivering
and
staring
at the moon

I Found God
for the Resurrection

somewhere between where you left me
standing on my grandmother's porch in the middle of fall
as the leaves gathered into piles

like the piles I used to jump in as a child
my cheeks and hands equally red
and steam rising from the coffee at the top of the steps

a smell that I can still remember
but not quite as potently as the smell of gasoline
a smell I thought I'd douse myself in
when I woke up in a demolished car and
walked down the road to the car that hit me
now in a tree
dead body inside

the smell of gasoline
which my father used to get paint
off of his hands

the smell that splashed on my pants
that I was awkwardly and constantly growing out of
while I mowed the lawn for someone else

and I've seen commercials that seem to say
that mowing the lawn on a Sunday with a beer
and a grilled burger you made yourself

is part of the American dream

and I wonder sometimes what the economy
did to my father's dreams
as I've seen them change for the 25
no wait
26 years I've known him

and sometimes I wonder if it was me that didn't turn out
the way that he wanted

or if it was him who didn't like the things his father liked
and he was the one who changed
because I don't think I did
and maybe I'm wrong

but listen

how will I explain this world to a child?
it's not as simple
as a young kid
wandering into a Pentecostal church service
snakes slithering
charmed or charred

but
suicide has been a fear all the way down the line
though not for me because I know my fears

I fear being cold

like the field I've mowed

but in winter
quiet and still
snow bright and constant
and the words I fear most
spilling over from the moon onto the ground
and washing over me in waves of anxiety
fear
anxiety
fear

and silence

[Untitled]

the fruit my father and I
picked when I was a child
        was bitter

            small brown apples
                    hard and meant for horses or deer

and pears
        sour and resistant

yet sometimes when I taste your lips
        I long for that fruit of my childhood

My Momma Don't Like You and She Likes Everyone
for Greg

      the smell of my grandmother's house
before the dementia took hold of her mind

          was somewhere between old and weak coffee
          and an often cleaned kitchen counter

and there are moments in my own home
where I mimic that smell
accidentally
but just for a moment
before it slips away
along with the memory of sitting at her
dining room table
watching the birds outside

I lost the poem I wanted to read
and I'm afraid
it was the best one that I've ever written
but now it's gone too

originally scribbled somewhere
with a splash of coffee on it

it was about coffee also
because of course it was

importantly it was about how my mother
sometimes made coffee for me in the mornings
despite the fact that she doesn't drink it
or know how it is supposed to taste

maybe because the same smell
that I remember fondly
in her mother's kitchen

reminds my mother of a different person
and one who was less kind

I suppose that my kindness varies too
when I think about things to break
over the head of the person in front of me
at the coffee shop
who ordered a drink that I couldn't remember the name of
if I tried

I say a drink because it's not a coffee
but I digress
or do I?

since ultimately
everything depends on the cup of coffee in Styrofoam
burnt
dumped out
on the way to hang drywall
on Father's Day

or the cup of coffee
that sat cold for three hours
in a diner in a college town
that you took a bus to

so we could talk and you could attend a party

I'm still not sure if you came to screw me
to screw me over
or because you knew we'd both cry when you walked away

and I saw you turn around
waiting for me to do the same
but I didn't

I walked away
knowing I was wrong
knowing I should have stayed
and then I had a coffee somewhere in Venice
when what I really wanted was wine

and a soft glow from a young woman
melts into the backdrop of summer grass
blowing blissfully in a breeze
that will not
and cannot stop
because the second that it stops moving
we fear that God has died

while we celebrate that God has risen
HE IS RISEN INDEED

we say that it is finished but
it sure doesn't seem like it is finished to me

because cracked and grease covered hands
praying for me
over a cup of coffee
first thing in the morning
make me wish that I had the soul of a man
who cries over his daughter growing up
and the people he can't save

For Hank

there is a woman somewhere
on this planet
who haunts me like a ghost

but damn your ghost
your Yorick and
those damned spots

but listen- if you loved me
would you know how I like my eggs?
and how I take my toast?

I guarantee that there's a God
and someday I'd take my son to church
only so his faith can waiver
because strong men question everything

am I still strong if I want a savior?
am I still strong if sometimes
I want to be held too?

there are phases that young
smart
strong men go through

those phases are accompanied by the spirit
attributed to J. Alfred Prufrock and
Edgar Allan Poe

as well as those fucking sonnets from John Keats
but not any of those books
or those movies
that blonde in college made me watch

my grandfather did think she was really pretty though

and this one time
she bought me

an Easter basket
with instant coffee in it
because she knew I drank Maxwell house
but she didn't know the difference

that same grandfather used to ask me
if I knew that the government was
poisoning us

I would tell him that I did not know that

but I know now
because love and life
are really always somehow enough
sometimes it hurts

to remember the woman who left you behind
while somewhere
your own home
waits empty
as a kind of payback

I cry at night sometimes
and that's none of your business

but she is in someone else's arms

while someone else's arms are bleeding
and bleach sits waiting

she knows not what she does
but she walks like
a punk song in a Mazda with a sun roof
and a girl who's been parking before

I know John Keats
and Homer
and I
slept alone that night

a lot of other nights too

while I read Chapman's Homer in its truest form
the form I don't give a fuck about

because Homer died
Keats died

who did they love and does it even matter
because fuck your legacy and
we have none

we have no legacy
we are not immortal

Ginsberg saw the best minds of his generation
pass before him
but the best of mine are right here right now
and there is nothing between us

and there is nothing better than what you want to do right now

and there is no one more beautiful than my mother
making coffee incorrectly
with bleary eyes
and two scoops too many
because she doesn't drink it
but wanted to make sure
I had coffee when I got up early the next day

we have no legacy
but we do have each other

Bromance (or One of the Lost Poems)

I'm in a hip coffee shop that's
too hip for a large coffee
because
they call it a grande

but listen

as I sit with a
book of Bukowski poems

this girl comes in
dressed in all black

some tights and a long
black shirt
that might be a dress

but I'm not quite sure and

when she walked
to the edge of the counter
to get her coffee

I spilled mine
all over my book

and by the time
I finished cleaning my
wasted
organic
free-trade
columbian
dark roast
red eye
pour-over coffee

she was walking outside
coffee in the air
like she had to balance herself

it's best that she left because
I noticed
as she got into her car
that she was wearing two different
socks

which is bad news if you ask me

so I went back to my book

and I'll tell you
I think that Bukowski had it hard for Hemingway

Nick Cannon Challenges Marshall Mathers to a Rap Battle

      a poem on a truckstop wall
gives the number for a prophet but
it was incorrect as dialed

and I can't remember the poem anymore

      somehow it revealed a deeper understanding
      of what it meant to be human

      it read like a Duchamp

I remember so little sometimes

only the outline of your curved side
in the early morning light of my first apartment and
the way a cup of tea warmed your hands through a sweater

      that prophet might have told me
      to find god

      in a handful of birdseed or
      in the taste of gin and tonic on your tongue

we might find god in the silence
that fills years and miles
or the empty space between your fingers

      and along the lines
      which my hands
      traced down your spine

About the Author

Wesley Scott McMasters is from rural Pennsylvania and always will be. He writes, teaches, and is an editor for *Red Flag Press*. He has a handful of poems and fiction pieces scattered across the internet and in a few print publications, including *Pennsylvania English*. He aspires to someday have a large garden and a full glass of good bourbon.

Gratitudes

Special thanks to my family, especially my parents, for their unending support, to the friends who have encouraged me, and to the poets, writers, musicians, and artists who never cease to amaze and inspire me, like Tony Vallone, Skysong, Henry Yukevich, AJ Schmitz, Pete Faziani, Matt Stumpf, Zach Fishel, Jason Mitchell, Jacob Kempfert, Brad Beauregard, Mitch James, John Dorsey, Nadia Zamin, Greg Ramkawsky, Jenna Ferraraccio, and all the wonderful wordsmiths who attend Lit Night at the Artist's Hand in Indiana, PA (and to Sandy Trimble, who makes the event possible). Thanks to Isaac Samay for making a coffee commensurate with my Monday morning misery to have on the front of the book. An especially big thank you to Amanda Oaks, whose poetry floors me, whose skills as an editor are unchallenged, and who made this project happen.

Notes and Acknowledgments

"Trying to Be a Person" comes from a phrase coined by Henry Yukevich.

"New Orleans Architecture" refers to the novel *V.* by Thomas Pynchon.

"Margot and the Nuclear So-Sos Sometimes Plays When I'm in the Local Coffee Shop, but this Poem Is Not about One of Their Songs" refers to and adapts a line from "That Dress Looks Nice On You" by Sufjan Stevens. The poem is after William Carlos Williams.

"DAILY AFFIRMATION" references and borrows a line from Jack Gilbert's "Failing and Flying." It also adapts a line from "The Love Song of J. Alfred Prufrock" by T. S. Eliot.

The title of "For AJ; or Why I Still Rock My Khakis with a Cuff and a Crease" borrows lyrics from "Still D.R.E." by Dr. Dre.

"3 Haiku for Late October" was published by *Red Flag Poetry* in March 2015.

"The Four Blood Moons" was published by *Words Dance* in September 2015 and references an apocalyptic belief based on Revelations 6:12. The poem borrows and adapts a line from "America" by Allen Ginsberg as well as a (different) line from "The Love Song of J. Alfred Prufrock."

"[Untitled]" on page 26 and "Girls with Coins" are slightly modified versions of poems to be published in the forthcoming issue of *Pennsylvania English*. The title "Girls with Coins" is adapted from "Boy with a Coin" by Iron & Wine.

"Upon Listening to Tool's 'Hooker with a Penis'" heavily calls on the work of Marcel Proust.

The title "My Momma Don't Like You and She Likes Everyone" is a borrowed lyric from "Love Yourself" by Justin Bieber.

The title "Nick Cannon Challenges Marshall Mathers to a Rap Battle" is adapted from the title of an article by Karli Bendlin published by the Huffington Post on June 6, 2016.

WORDS DANCE PUBLISHING has one aim:

To spread mind-blowing / heart-opening poetry.

Words Dance artfully & carefully wrangles words that were born to dance wildly in the heart-mind matrix. Rich, edgy, raw, emotionally-charged energy balled up & waiting to whip your eyes wild; we rally together words that were written to make your heart go boom right before they slay your mind.

Words Dance Publishing is an independent press out of Pennsylvania. We work closely & collaboratively with all of our writers to ensure that their words continue to breathe in a sound & stunning home. Most importantly though, we leave the windows in these homes unlocked so you, the reader, can crawl in & throw one fuck of a house party.

To learn more about our books, authors, events & Words Dance Poetry Magazine, visit:

WORDSDANCE.COM

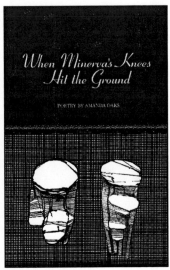

FREE PDF EBOOKS

WHERE'D YOU PUT THE KEYS GIRL + WHEN MINERVA'S KNEES HIT THE GROUND
Poetry by Amanda Oaks

DOWNLOAD HERE:

http://wordsdance.com/free-stuff

Music-inspired digital chapbooks by *Words Dance* Founder, Amanda Oaks. These collections were made with deep love & respect for Tori Amos' + Deftones' music & are made up of erasure poems created from select songs from each artist's catalog + each of the erasure poems are paired an original sister poem & the title of that sister poem is a short lyric from the songs chosen.

"Oaks' original poems, which accompany the erasures, are among the best of her work to date. They are urgent and striking. This is the work of a fully confident poet hitting her stride."
— **KENDALL A. BELL**
Publisher/Editor @ *Maverick Duck Press*

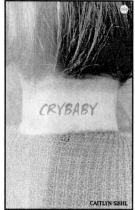

Crybaby by Caitlyn Siehl

No Matter the Time by Fortesa Latifi

The Goddess Songs by Azra Tabassum

Why I'm Not Where You Are by Brianna Albers

Before the First Kiss by Ashe Vernon & Trista Mateer

Our Bodies & Other Fine Machines by Natalie Wee

holyFool by Amanda Oaks

A FIELD OF BLOOMING BRUISES
Poetry by Schuyler Peck

| $12 | 58 pages | 5.5" x 8.5" | softcover |

ISBN: 978-0692628591

To my first year of recovery, my first impression was wrong, you turned out much sweeter than I thought. To my followers, who inspire me daily with their kindness; for all the friends I haven't met yet. To my friends, you are every light I've ever looked for. To my Tyler, for giving me enough love, I can fill books with it.

"Peck's poems carry both a lovely fragility and a sense of strength, and it is a testament to her prowess as a poet that she comes out of her trials all that much stronger because of it. While some poems here are stronger than others, nothing here is boring or ordinary. There is a warmth to Peck's words, and she wears her soft nature with no sense of shame. You could lump her in with similar poets like Clementine Von Radics and Charlotte Erikkson, but she's better than both of them, and has the potential to be one of the best contemporary poets, in time."

— **KENDALL A. BELL**
Publisher/Editor @ *Maverick Duck Press*

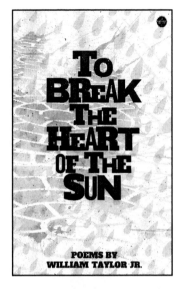

TO BREAK THE HEART OF THE SUN
Poetry by William Taylor Jr.

| $15 | 132 pages | 5.5" x 8.5" | softcover |

ISBN: 978-0692617380

"*In To Break the Heart of the Sun* Taylor invites you over for a few drinks & then takes you out on the gritty streets of San Francisco. You dip into the bars & cafés in the Tenderloin & North Beach, you skirt the sidewalks down Haight, in Chinatown & the Mission, all the while bonding over the people you love, music, poetry, past loves, friendship, your childhoods & dreams. You question life, both the dark & light of it, looking for the truth of it. You laugh & weep with the people you meet along the way, every face some kind of prayer. Taylor teaches you how to dance with your joy while dressed in your sorrow. He has a way of showing you how keep your heart open & closed at the same time so you don't lose your footing, but if you do, with kind eyes & laughter escaping both your lips, his hand reaches down to help you up."

"William Taylor, Jr, my pick for best poet in San Francisco, is back with *To Break the Heart of the Sun*, and it's every bit a Taylor book, every bit as sad, and beautiful, and even begrudgingly hopeful as all his best work. Or, if not hopeful, that at least graceful in its wise and simple acceptance of the silly problem called life. His lines crackle and sing, sweeping through the crumbling landscape of the Tenderloin, and the vast, Buddha-like landscape of his inner life. These poems will save something otherwise lost even as we fumbling, stuttering mortals fade...and I can think of no higher honor than that. And Amanda at Words Dance has put together a drop-dead gorgeous book, with cover-art on par with those sublime Black Sparrow covers of years past...so there is absolutely nothing but praise for this entire glorious project. Treat yourself to a copy!"

— HOSHO MCCREESH
Author of *A Deep and Gorgeous Thirst*

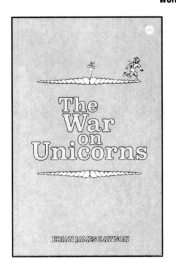

THE WAR ON UNICORNS
Poetry by Brian James Dawson

| $12 | 74 pages | 5.5" x 8.5" | softcover |

ISBN: 978-0692487754

"*The War on Unicorns*, with its parts 1 through 40, which from its opening lines- *The dog barks constantly. Shining men in / riot gear accept flowers.* – enters the conflicting imaginations of the local and the empyreal. The book itself is a halcyonian triumph. Lines, of course, abound. *A paper airplane flies towards a furnace* (2). *A remade red dress / hangs lugubriously on a wooden rack / in a closet left over from / the Mormon migration* (5). But I've said too much of what it merely says. It doesn't build, it contains, it is house. Inside, there is map enough to distract the bombings. At one point, Dawson directs us to *Remember Tehran*. It is not jarring, it is just the end of a poem. Dawson is a student of history but teaches the sane myth."

— **BARTON SMOCK**

Author of *Misreckon* & *The Blood You Don't See Is Fake*

"The poems in *The War on Unicorns* are perfect examples of the best words in the best order. I love the snap-shot feel of each poem, and if a picture is worth a thousand words, then these word-pictures are golden. *Piles/of old newspapers /yellow in the long light/of a sequester sun* and *he wishes-wishes to retract all his lies / and rake them into multi-colored piles.* The observation of human experiences and relationships are sharp - *I am the curator of the universe's / museum of cruel jokes.* This writing has both style and substance. *Take off your armor; unlock your heart* - you should buy this book."

— **VIOLET WILD**

WHAT WE BURIED
Poetry by Caitlyn Siehl

| $12 | 64 pages | 5.5" x 8.5" | softcover |

ISBN: 978-0615985862

GOODREADS CHOICE AWARD NOMINEE FOR POETRY (2014)

This book is a cemetery of truths buried alive. The light draws you in where you will find Caitlyn there digging. When you get close enough, she'll lean in & whisper, Baby, buried things will surface no matter what, get to them before they get to you first. Her unbounded love will propel you to pick up a shovel & help— even though the only thing you want to do is kiss her lips, kiss her hands, kiss every one of her stretch marks & the fire that is raging in pit of her stomach. She'll see your eyes made of devour & sadness, she'll hug you & say, Baby, if you eat me alive, I will cut my way out of your stomach. Don't let this be your funeral. Teach yourself to navigate the wound.

"It takes a true poet to write of love and desire in a way that manages to surprise and excite. Caitlyn Siehl does this in poem after poem and makes it seem effortless. Her work shines with a richness of language and basks in images that continue to delight and astound with multiple readings. *What We Buried* is a treasure from cover to cover."

— WILLIAM TAYLOR JR.
Author of *An Age of Monsters*

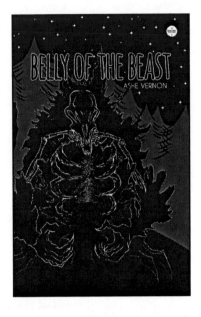

BELLY OF THE BEAST
Poetry by Ashe Vernon

| $12 | 82 pages | 5.5" x 8.5" | softcover |

ISBN: 978-0692300541

"Into the *Belly of the Beast* we crawl with Ashe as our guide; into the dark visceral spaces where love, lust, descent and desire work their transformative magic and we find ourselves utterly altered in the reading. A truly gifted poet and truth-spiller, Ashe's metaphors create images within images, leading us to question the subjective truths, both shared and hidden, in personal relationship – to the other, and to oneself. Unflinching in her approach, her poetry gives voice to that which most struggle to admit – even if only to themselves. And as such, *Belly of the Beast* is a work of startling courage and rich depth – a darkly delicious pleasure."

— AMY PALKO
Goddess Guide, Digital Priestess & Writer

"It isn't often you find a book of poetry that is as unapologetic, as violent, as moving as this one. Ashe's writing is intense and visceral. You feel the punch in your gut while you're reading, but you don't question it. You know why it's there and you almost welcome it."

— CAITLYN SIEHL
Author of *What We Buried*

"The poems you are about to encounter are the fierce time capsules of girl-hood, girded with sharp elbows, surprise kisses, the meanders of wander-lust. We need voices this strong, this true for the singing reminds us that we are not alone, that someone, somewhere is listening for the faint pulse that is our wish to be seen. Grab hold, this voice will be with us forever."

— RA WASHINGTON
GuidetoKulchurCleveland.com

DOWRY MEAT

Poetry by Heather Knox

| $12 | 110 pages | 5.5" x 8.5" | softcover |

ISBN: 978-0692398494

Heather Knox's *Dowry Meat* is a gorgeous, tough-as-nails debut that arrives on your doorstep hungry and full of dark news. There's damage here, and obsession, and more haunted beauty in the wreckage of just about everything—relationships, apartment clutter, rough sex, the body, and of course the just-post apocalypse— than you or I could hope to find on our own. These are poems that remind us not that life is hard—that's old news—but that down there in the gravel and broken glass is where the truth-worth-hearing lies, and maybe the life worth living. If you were a city, Knox tells us, unflinching as always, *I'd… read your graffiti. Drink your tap water./Feel your smog and dirt stick to my sweat… If you were a city, I'd expect to be robbed.*

— **JON LOOMIS**

Author of *Vanitas Motel (winner of the FIELD prize)* and *The Pleasure Principle*

"Heather Knox's debut collection is a lyric wreath made of purulent ribbon and the most inviting of thorns. Tansy and tokophobia, lachrymosity and lavage are braided together in this double collection, which marries a sci-fi Western narrative to a lyric sequence. Both elapse in an impossible location made of opposites—futuristic nostalgia, or erotic displeasure—otherwise known as the universe in which we (attempt to) live."

— **JOYELLE MCSWEENEY**

Author of *The Necropastoral: Poetry, Media, Occults & Salamandrine: 8 Gothics*

"*Dowry Meat*'s apocalyptic fever dream myth-making bleeds into what we might call the poetry of witness or the tradition of the confessional, except that these lines throb with lived experience and a body isn't necessarily a confession. Heather Knox's poems are beautifully wrought and beautifully raw."

— **DORA MALECH**

Author of *Shore Ordered Ocean & Say So*

Other titles available from
WORDS DANCE PUBLISHING

THE NO YOU NEVER LISTENED TO
Poetry by Meggie Royer

| $14 | 142 pages | 5.5" x 8.5" | softcover |

ISBN: 978-0692463635

"It's a strange thing when the highest praise you can offer for someone's work is, "I wish this didn't exist," but that was the refrain that echoed in my head after I read Meggie Royer's third book.

As fans of her work know, Meggie takes the universal and makes it personal. With *The No You Never Listened To*, she takes the personal and makes it universal. As a sexual assault survivor, Meggie is well-acquainted with trauma: the aftermath, the guilt, the anger. She has never shied away from taking Hemingway's advice – write hard and clear about what hurts – and that strength has never been more of an asset than with this body of work.

The No You Never Listened To is the book you will wish you'd had when trauma climbed into your bed. It is the book you will give to friends who are dragged from their "before" into a dark and terrifying "after". And yes, it is the book you will wish didn't exist.

But it is also the one that will remind you, in your darkest moments, where the blame really belongs. It will remind you that your memory will not always be an enemy. And it will remind you that none of us have ever been alone in this."

— CLAIRE BIGGS
To Write Love on Her Arms Editor / Writer

"Nietzsche once warned us to be careful gazing into the abyss, that we run the risk of staring so long that the void consumes us. The poems in this book were born of the abyss, of conflict & trauma & survival. And through these poems, Meggie Royer stares – hard, unflinching, courageous – and instead of gazing back, the abyss looks away."

— WILLIAM JAMES
Drunk In A Midnight Choir editor & author of *rebel hearts & restless ghosts*

CHLOE

Poetry by Kristina Haynes

| $12 | 110 pages | 5.5" x 8.5" | softcover |

ISBN: 978-0692386637

Chloe is brave and raw, adolescence mixed with salt. These poems are about how hungry we've been, how foolish, how lonely. Chloe is not quite girl nor woman, full of awkward bravery. Kristina is an electric voice that pulls Chloe apart page after page, her heartbreaks, her too many drinks, her romantic experiences of pleasure and pain. Chloe and Kristina make a perfect team to form an anthem for girls everywhere, an anthem that reassures us we deserve to take up space. Indeed, when I met Chloe, I too thought "This is the closest I've been to anybody in months."

— **MEGGIE ROYER**

Author of *Survival Songs*
and *Healing Old Wounds with New Stitches*

"*Chloe* is one of the most intimate books you'll read all year. Chloe is my new best friend. I want to eat burnt popcorn on her couch and watch Friends reruns. I want to borrow her clothing, write on her walls in lipstick. Chloe is not your dream girl. She doesn't have everything figured out. She's messy. She's always late. She promises old lovers she'll never call again. She teaches you what the word "indulgence" means. She's wonderful, wonderful, wonderful. In *Chloe*, Kristina Haynes digs into the grittiness of modern womanhood, of mothers and confusion and iPhones and two, maybe three-night-stands. Her truths are caramels on the tongue but are blunter, harsher on the way down. Kristina introduces us to a character I'll be thinking about for a very long time. Go read this book. Then write a poem. Then kiss someone. Then buy an expensive strain of tea and a new pillow. Then go read it again."

— **YASMIN BELKHYR**

Editor-in-Chief at *Winter Tangerine Review*

LITERARY SEXTS
VOLUME 2

A Collection of Short & Sexy Love Poems

| $12 | 76 pages | 5.5" x 8.5" | softcover |

ISBN: 978-0692359594

This is the highly anticipated second volume of Literary Sexts! After over 1,000 copies of Literary Sexts Volume 1 being sold, we are super-excited to bring you a second volume! Literary Sexts is an annual modern day anthology of short love & sexy poems edited by Amanda Oaks & Caitlyn Siehl. These are poems that you would text to your lover. Poems that you would slip into a back pocket, suitcase, wallet or purse on the sly. Poems that you would write on slips of paper & stick under your crush's windshield wiper or pillow. Poems that you would write on a Post-it note & leave on the bathroom mirror. Poems that you would whisper into your lover's ear. Hovering around 40 contributors & 130 poems, this book reads is like one long & very intense conversation between two lovers. It's absolutely breathtaking.

This is for the leather
& the lace of you—

your flushed cheeks
& what set them ablaze.

POEM YOUR HEART OUT
Prompts, Poems & Room to Add Your Own
Volume 1

| $15 | 158 pages | 5.5" x 8.5" | softcover |

ISBN: 978-0692317464

PROMPT BOOK • ANTHOLOGY • WORKBOOK

Words Dance Publishing teamed up with the Writer's Digest's Poetic Asides blog to make their Poem-A-Day challenge this year even more spectacular!

Part poetry prompt book, part anthology of the best poems written during the 2014 April PAD(Poem-A-Day) Challenge on the Poetic Asides blog (by way of Writer's Digest) & part workbook, let both, the prompt & poem, inspire you to create your own poetic masterpieces. Maybe you participated in April & want to document your efforts during the month. Maybe you're starting now, like so many before you, with just a prompt, an example poem, & an invitation to poem your heart out! You're encouraged—heck, dared—to write your own poems inside of this book!

This book is sectioned off by Days, each section will hold the prompt for that day, the winning poem for that day & space for you to place the poem you wrote for that day's prompt inside.

Just a few of the guest judges: Amy King, Bob Hicok, Jericho Brown, Nate Pritts, Kristina Marie Darling & Nin Andrews...

Challenge yourself, your friend, a writing workshop or your class to this 30 Day Poem-A-Day Challenge!

THIS IS AN INVITATION TO POEM YOUR HEART OUT!

I EAT CROW + BLUE COLLAR AT BEST
Poetry by Amanda Oaks + Zach Fishel

| $15 | 124 pages | 5.5" x 8.5" | softcover |

Home is where the heart is and both poets' hearts were raised in the Appalachian region of Western Pennsylvania surrounded by coal mines, sawmills, two-bit hotel taverns, farms, churches and cemeteries. These poems take that region by the throat and shake it until it's bloody and then, they breathe it back to life. This book is where you go when you're looking for nostalgia to kick you in the teeth. This is where you go when you're 200 miles away from a town you thought you'd never want to return to but suddenly you're pining for it.

Amanda and Zach grew up 30 miles from each other and met as adults through poetry. Explore both the male and female perspective of what it's like to grow up hemmed in by an area's economic struggle. These poems mine through life, love, longing and death, they're for home and away, and the inner strength that is not deterred by any of those things.

SPLIT BOOK #1

What are Split Books?

Two full-length books from two poets in one + there's a collaborative split between the poets in the middle!

SHAKING THE TREES
Poetry by Azra Tabassum

| $12 | 72 pages | 5.5" x 8.5" | softcover |

ISBN: 978-0692232408

From the very first page *Shaking the Trees* meets you at the edge of the forest, extends a limb & seduces you into taking a walk through the dark & light of connection. Suddenly, like a gunshot in the very-near distance, you find yourself traipsing though a full-blown love story that you can't find your way out of because the story is actually the landscape underneath your feet. It's okay though, you won't get lost– you won't go hungry. Azra shakes every tree along the way so their fruit blankets the ground before you. She picks up pieces & hands them to you but not before she shows you how she can love you so gently it will feel like she's unpeeling you carefully from yourself. She tells you that it isn't about the bite but the warm juice that slips from the lips down chin. She holds your hand when you're trudging through the messier parts, shoes getting stuck in the muck of it all, but you'll keep going with the pulp of the fruit still stuck in-between your teeth, the juice will dry in the crooks of your elbows & in the lines on your palms. You'll taste bittersweet for days.

"I honestly haven't read a collection like this before, or at least I can't remember having read one. My heart was wrecked by Azra. It's like that opening line in Fahrenheit 451 when Bradbury says, "It was a pleasure to burn." It really was a pleasure being wrecked by it."

— **NOURA**
of *NouraReads*

"I wanted to cry and cheer and fuck. I wanted to take the next person I saw and kiss them straight on the lips and say, "Remember this moment for the rest of your life."

— **CHELSEA MILLER**

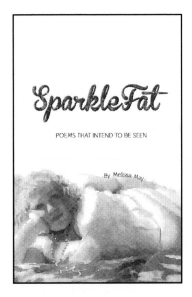

SparkleFat

POEMS THAT INTEND TO BE SEEN

By Melissa May

SPARKLEFAT
Poetry by Melissa May

| \$12 | 62 pages | 5.5" x 8.5" | softcover |

SparkleFat is a loud, unapologetic, intentional book of poetry about my body, about your body, about fat bodies and how they move through the world in every bit of their flash and spark and burst. Some of the poems are painful, some are raucous celebrations, some are reminders and love letters and quiet gifts back to the vessel that has traveled me so gracefully - some are a hymnal of yes, but all of them sparkle. All of them don't mind if you look – really. They built their own house of intention, and they draped that shit in lime green sequins. All of them intend to be seen. All of them have no more fucks to give about a world that wants them to be quiet.

"I didn't know how much I needed this book until I found myself, three pages in, ugly crying on the plane next to a concerned looking business man. This book is the most glorious, glittery pink permission slip. It made me want to go on a scavenger hunt for every speck of shame in my body and sing hot, sweaty R&B songs to it. There is no voice more authentic, generous and resounding than Melissa May. From her writing, to her performance, to her role in the community she delivers fierce integrity & staggering passion. From the first time I watched her nervously step to the mic, to the last time she crushed me in a slam, it is has been an honor to watch her astound the poetry slam world and inspire us all to be not just better writers but better people. We need her."

— LAUREN ZUNIGA
Author of *The Smell of Good Mud*

"*SparkleFat* is a firework display of un-shame. Melissa May's work celebrates all of the things we have been so long told deserved no streamers. This collection invites every fat body out to the dance and steams up the windows in the backseat of the car afterwards by kissing the spots we thought (or even hoped) no one noticed but are deserving of love just the same as our mouths."

— RACHEL WILEY
Author of *Fat Girl Finishing School*

LOVE AND OTHER SMALL WARS

Poetry by Donna-Marie Riley

| $12 | 76 pages | 5.5" x 8.5" | softcover |

ISBN: 978-0615931111

Love and Other Small Wars reminds us that when you come back from combat usually the most fatal of wounds are not visible. Riley's debut collection is an arsenal of deeply personal poems that embody an intensity that is truly impressive yet their hands are tender. She enlists you. She gives you camouflage & a pair of boots so you can stay the course through the minefield of her heart. You will track the lovely flow of her soft yet fierce voice through a jungle of powerful imagery on womanhood, relationships, family, grief, sexuality & love, amidst other matters. Battles with the heart aren't easily won but Riley hits every mark. You'll be relieved that you're on the same side. Much like war, you'll come back from this book changed.

"Riley's work is wise, intense, affecting, and uniquely crafted. This collection illuminates her ability to write with both a gentle hand and a bold spirit. She inspires her readers and creates an indelible need inside of them to consume more of her exceptional poetry. I could read *Love and Other Small Wars* all day long…and I did."

— **APRIL MICHELLE BRATTEN**
editor of *Up the Staircase Quarterly*

"Riley's poems are personal, lyrical and so vibrant they practically leap off the page, which also makes them terrifying at times. A beautiful debut."

— **BIANCA STEWART**

LITERARY SEXTS

A Collection of Short & Sexy Love Poems
(Volume 1)

| $12 | 42 pages | 5.5" x 8.5" | softcover |

ISBN: 978-0615959726

Literary Sexts is a modern day anthology of short love poems with subtle erotic undertones edited by Amanda Oaks & Caitlyn Siehl. Hovering around 50 contributors & 124 poems, this book reads is like one long & very intense conversation between two lovers. It's absolutely breathtaking. These are poems that you would text to your lover. Poems that you would slip into a back pocket, suitcase, wallet or purse on the sly. Poems that you would write on slips of paper & stick under your crush's windshield wiper. Poems that you would write on a Post-it note & leave on the bathroom mirror.

HIT #1
ON AMAZON'S
HOT NEW
RELEASE LIST!

"It's like 100+ new ways to make a reader blush. The imagery is so subtle yet completely thrilling..." **NOW I NEED A COLD SHOWER!"**
- K. W.

"**I DEVOURED IT!** I physically wanted to eat these poems. I wanted to wear them on my skin like perfume..."
- A. G.

"I have consumed this in ways that have left my insides looking like strips of velvet fabric... **SO ORGASMIC!"**
- K. B.

"**A MAELSTROM OF EMOTIONS!** I only hope that there is a Volume 2, a Volume 3 and so on because I need more of this!"
- Daniel CZ.

Unrequited love? We've all been there.

Enter:

WHAT TO DO AFTER SHE SAYS NO
by Kris Ryan.

This skillfully designed 10-part poem explores what it's like to ache for someone. This is the book you buy yourself or a friend when you are going through a breakup or a one-sided crush, it's the perfect balance between aha, humor & heartbreak.

WHAT TO DO AFTER SHE SAYS NO
A Poem by Kris Ryan

$10 | 104 pages | 5" x 8" | softcover | ISBN: 978-0615870045

"*What to Do After She Says No* takes us from Shanghai to the interior of a refrigerator, but mostly dwells inside the injured human heart, exploring the aftermath of emotional betrayal. This poem is a compact blast of brutality, with such instructions as "Climb onto the roof and jump off. If you break your leg, you are awake. If you land without injury, pinch and twist at your arm until you wake up." Ryan's use of the imperative often leads us to a reality where pain is the only outcome, but this piece is not without tenderness, and certainly not without play, with sounds and images ricocheting off each other throughout. Anticipate the poetry you wish you knew about during your last bad breakup; this poem offers a first "foothold to climb out" from that universal experience."

— **LISA MANGINI**

"Reading Kris Ryan's *What To Do After She Says No* is like watching your heart pound outside of your chest. Both an unsettling visual experience and a hurricane of sadness and rebirth—this book demands more than just your attention, it takes a little bit of your soul, and in the end, makes everything feel whole again."

— **JOHN DORSEY**
author of ***Tombstone Factory***

"*What to Do After She Says No* is exquisite. Truly, perfectly exquisite. It pulls you in on a familiar and wild ride of a heart blown open and a mind twisting in an effort to figure it all out. It's raw and vibrant...and in the same breath comforting. I want to crawl inside this book and live in a world where heartache is expressed so magnificently.

— **JO ANNA ROTHMAN**
MA, Coach & Conjurer of Electric Creative Wholeness

NO GLASS
ALLOWED

Poems by Tammy Foster Brewer

Tammy Foster Brewer is the type of poet who makes me wish I could write poetry instead of novels. From motherhood to love to work, Tammy's poems highlight the extraordinary in the ordinary and leave the reader wondering how he did not notice what was underneath all along. I first heard Tammy read 'The Problem is with Semantics' months ago, and it's stayed with me ever since. Now that I've read the entire collection, I only hope I can make room to keep every one of her poems in my heart and mind tomorrow and beyond.

— NICOLE ROSS, author

NO GLASS ALLOWED
Poetry by Tammy Foster Brewer

$12 | 56 pages | 6" x 9" | softcover | ISBN: 978-0615870007

Brewer's collection is filled with uncanny details that readers will wear like the accessories of womanhood. Fishing the Chattahoochee, sideways trees, pollen on a car, white dresses and breast milk, and so much more -- all parts of a deeply intellectual pondering of what is often painful and human regarding the other halves of mothers and daughters, husbands and wives, lovers and lost lovers, children and parents.

— NICHOLAS BELARDES
author of *Songs of the Glue Machines*

Tammy deftly juxtaposes distinct imagery with stories that seem to collide in her brilliant poetic mind. Stories of transmissions and trees and the words we utter, or don't. Of floods and forgiveness, conversations and car lanes, bread and beginnings, awe and expectations, desire and leaps of faith that leave one breathless, and renewed.

"When I say I am a poet / I mean my house has many windows" has to be one of the best descriptions of what it's like to be a contemporary female poet who not only holds down a day job and raises a family, but whose mind and heart regularly file away fleeting images and ideas that might later be woven into something permanent, and perhaps even beautiful. This ability is not easily acquired. It takes effort, and time, and the type of determination only some writers, like Tammy, possess and are willing to actively exercise.

— KAREN DEGROOT CARTER
author of *One Sister's Song*

DO YOU WRITE POETRY?

Submit it to our biweekly online magazine!

We publish poems every Tuesday & Thursday on website.

Come see what all the fuss is about!

We like Poems that sneak up on you. Poems that make out with you. Poems that bloody your mouth just to kiss it clean. Poems that bite your cheek so you spend all day tonguing the wound. Poems that vandalize your heart. Poems that act like a tin can phone connecting you to your childhood. Fire Alarm Poems. Glitterbomb Poems. Jailbreak Poems. Poems that could marry the land or the sea; that are both the hero & the villain. Poems that are the matches when there is a city-wide power outage. Poems that throw you overboard just dive in & save your ass. Poems that push you down on the stoop in front of history's door screaming at you to knock. Poems that are soft enough to fall asleep on. Poems that will still be clinging to the walls inside of your bones on your 90th birthday. We like poems. Submit yours.

WORDSDANCE.COM